Majestic
Horses
Deluxe
Journal

"When I bestride him, I soar,
I am a hawk: he trots the air;
the earth sings when he touches it;
the basest horn of his hoof is more
musical than the pipe of Hermes."

- William Shakespeare

Royal Horse Press
Deluxe Designs

Deluxe Horse Journal
Belonging To:

_____

"God forbid that I should go to any
Heaven in which there are no horses."

- R.B. Cunninghame Graham

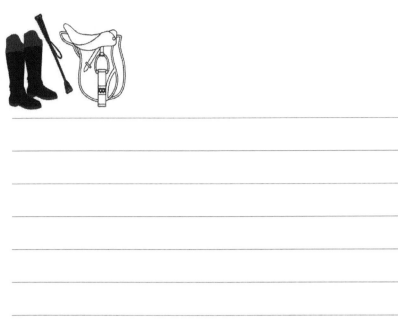

Made in the USA
Las Vegas, NV
08 March 2021